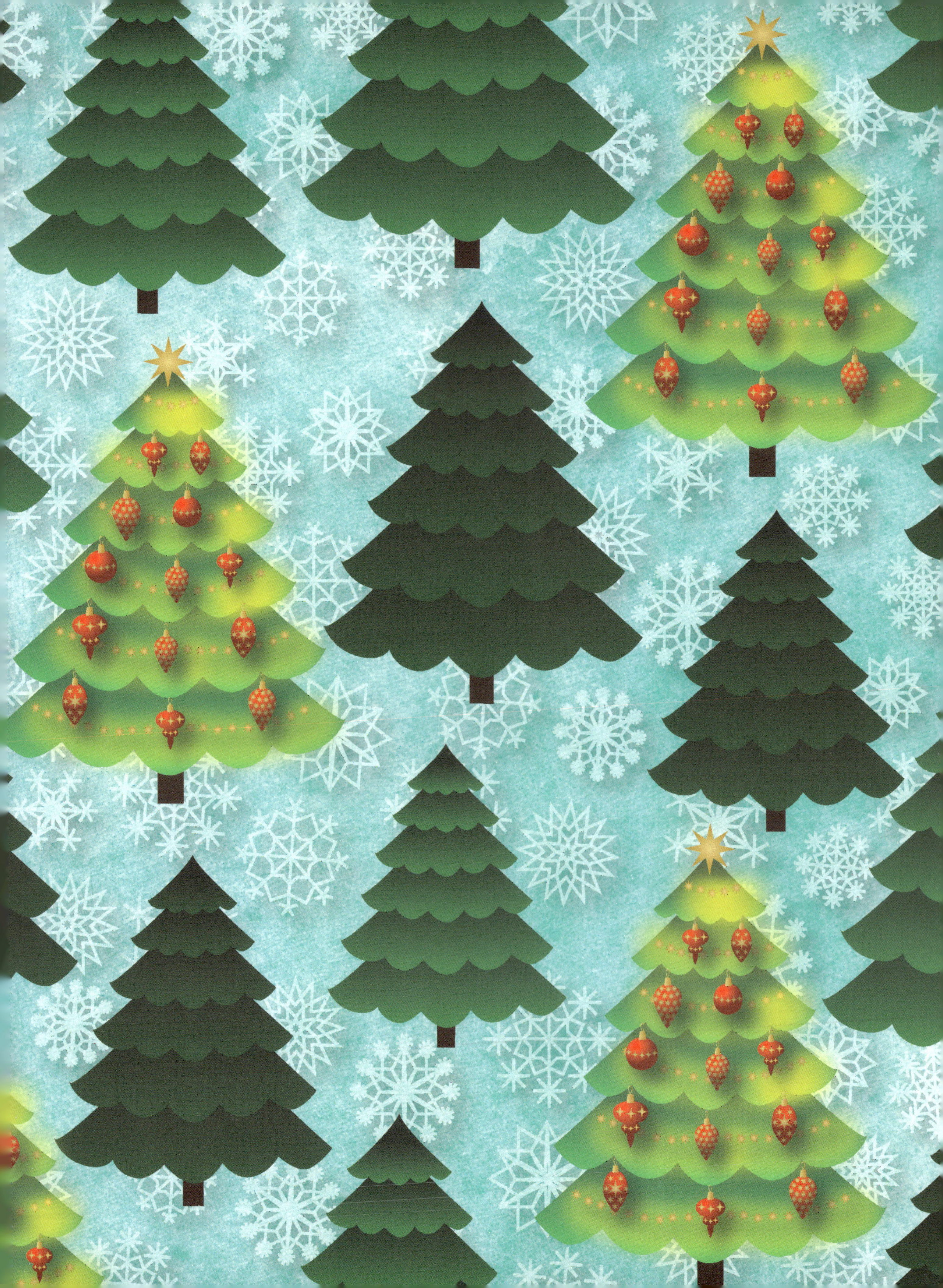

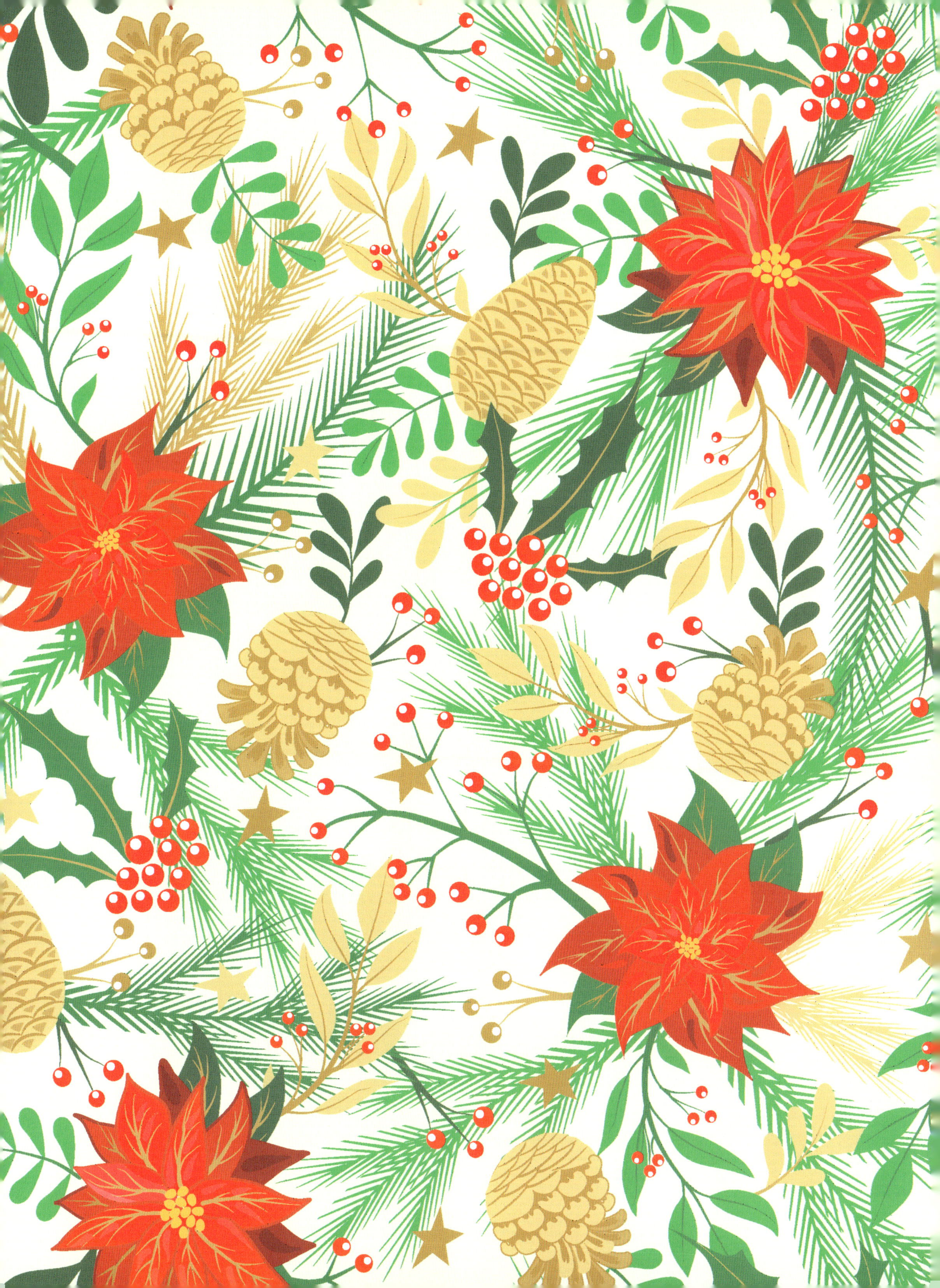

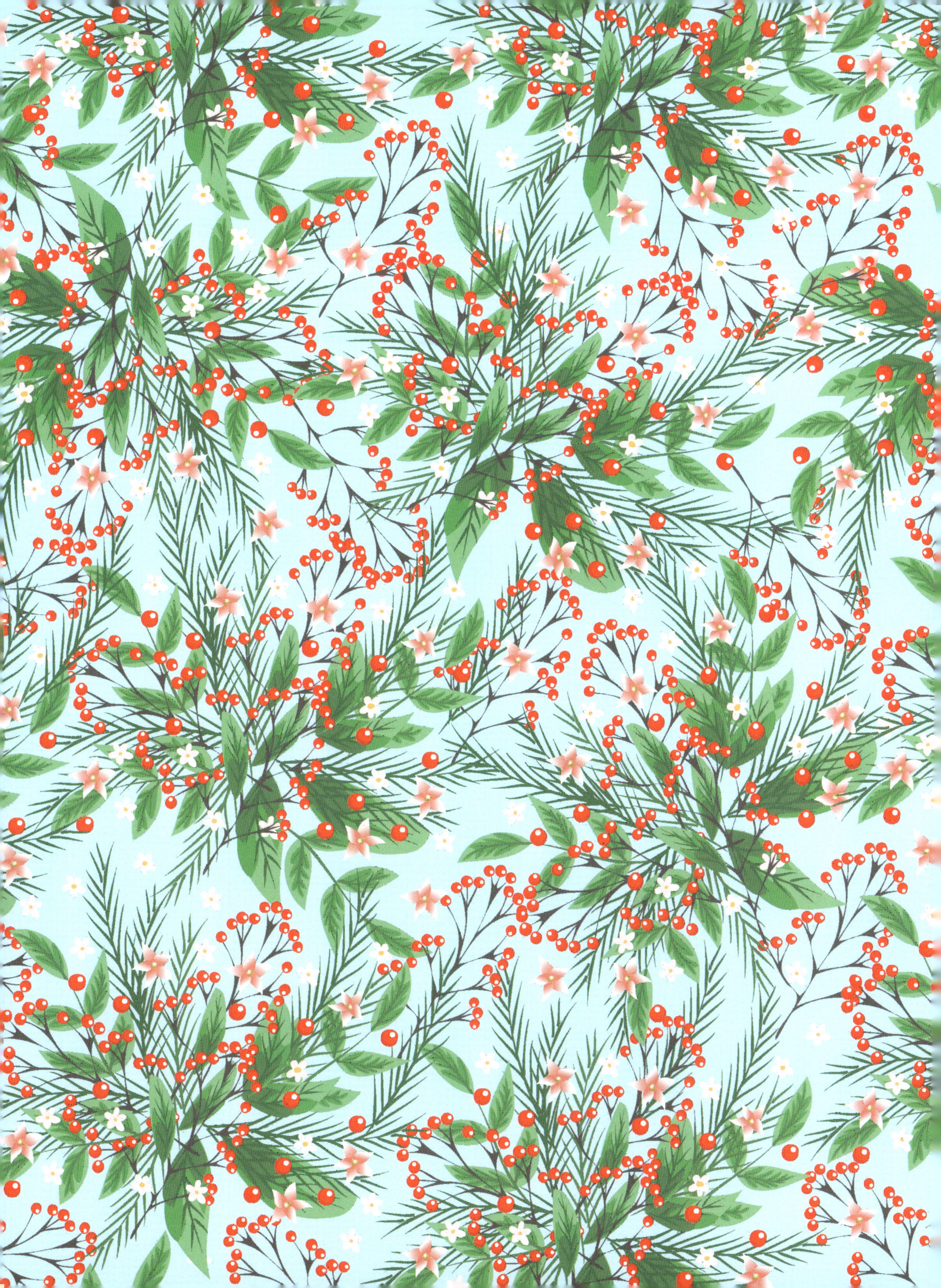

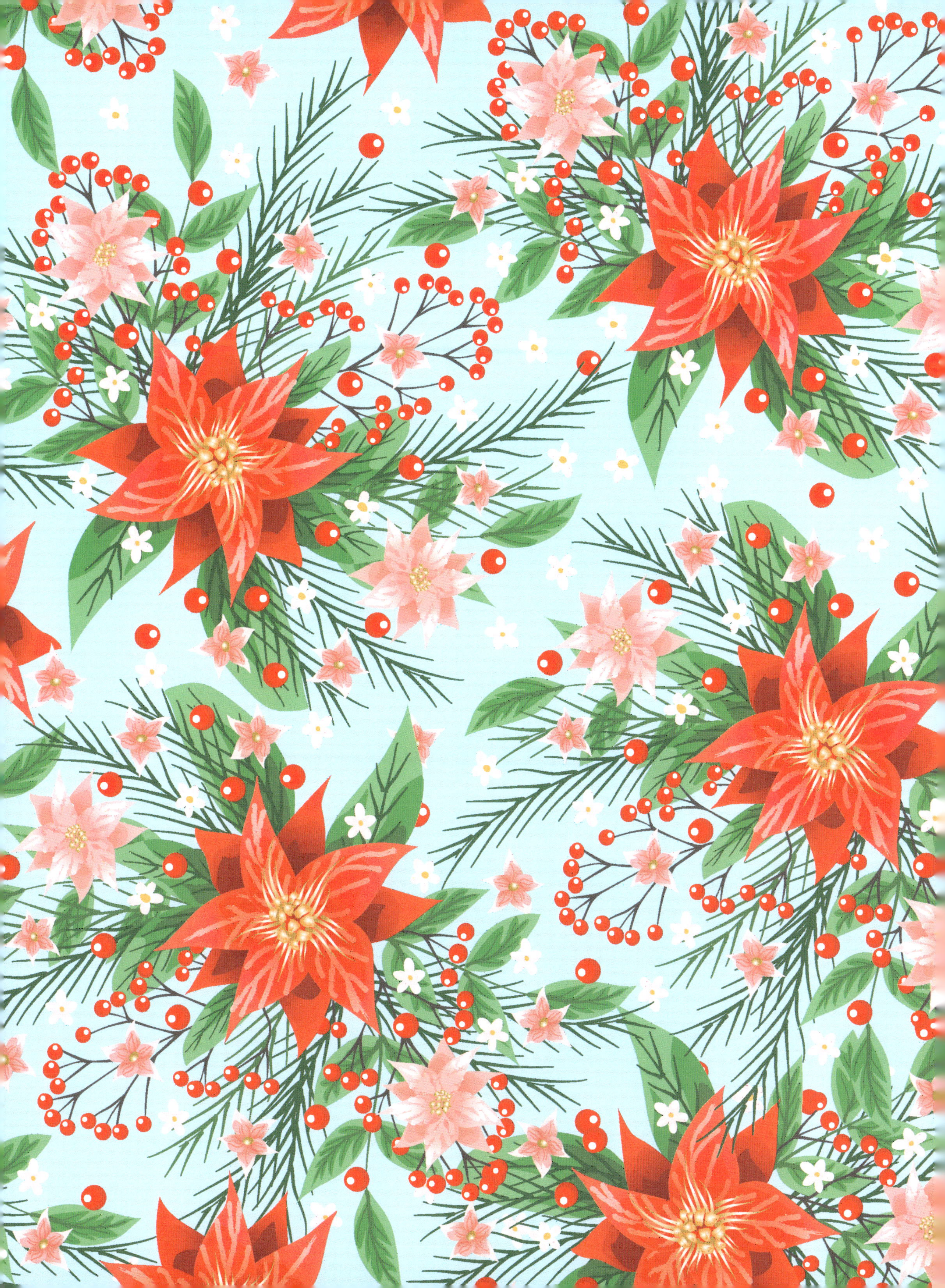

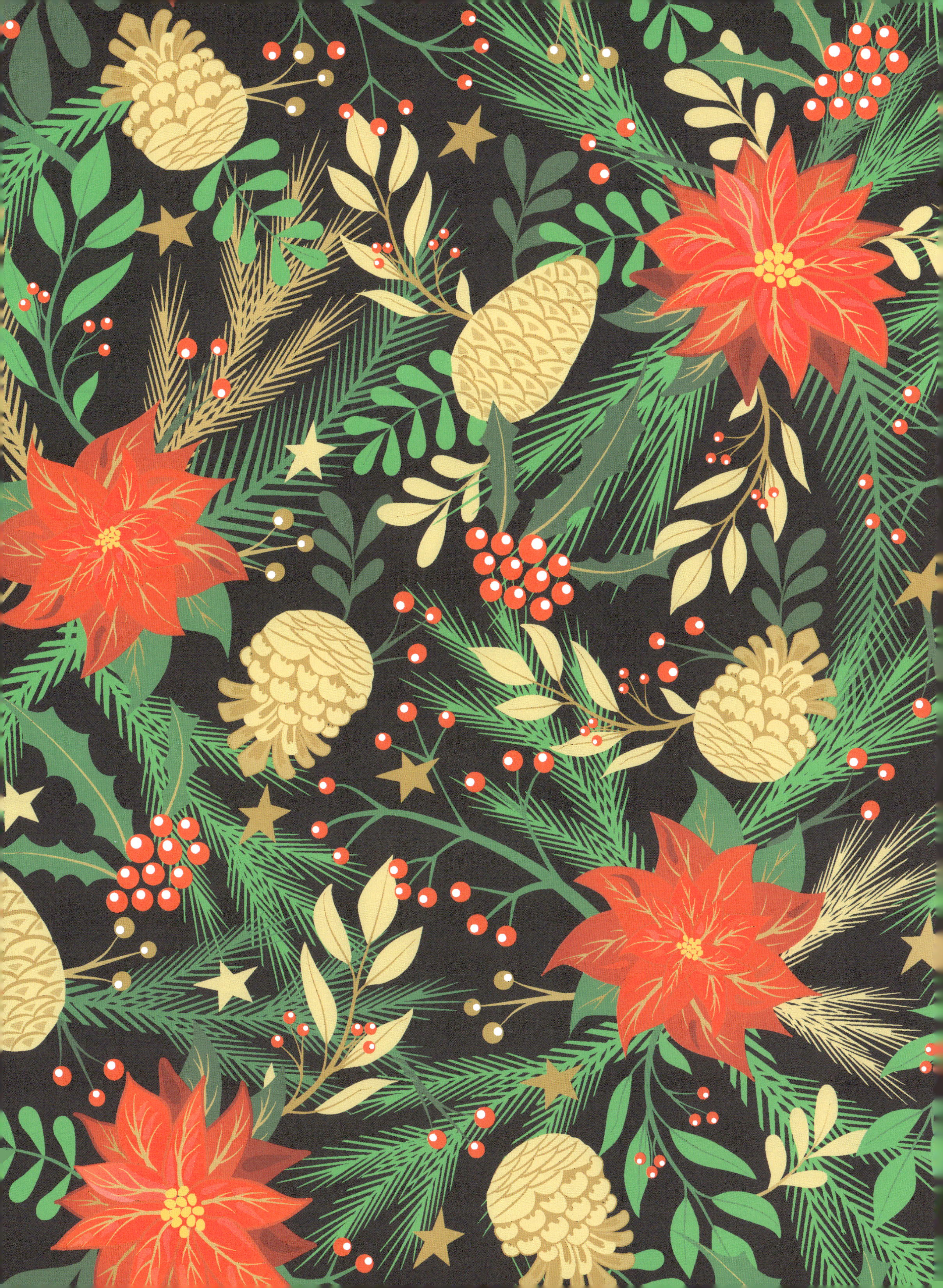

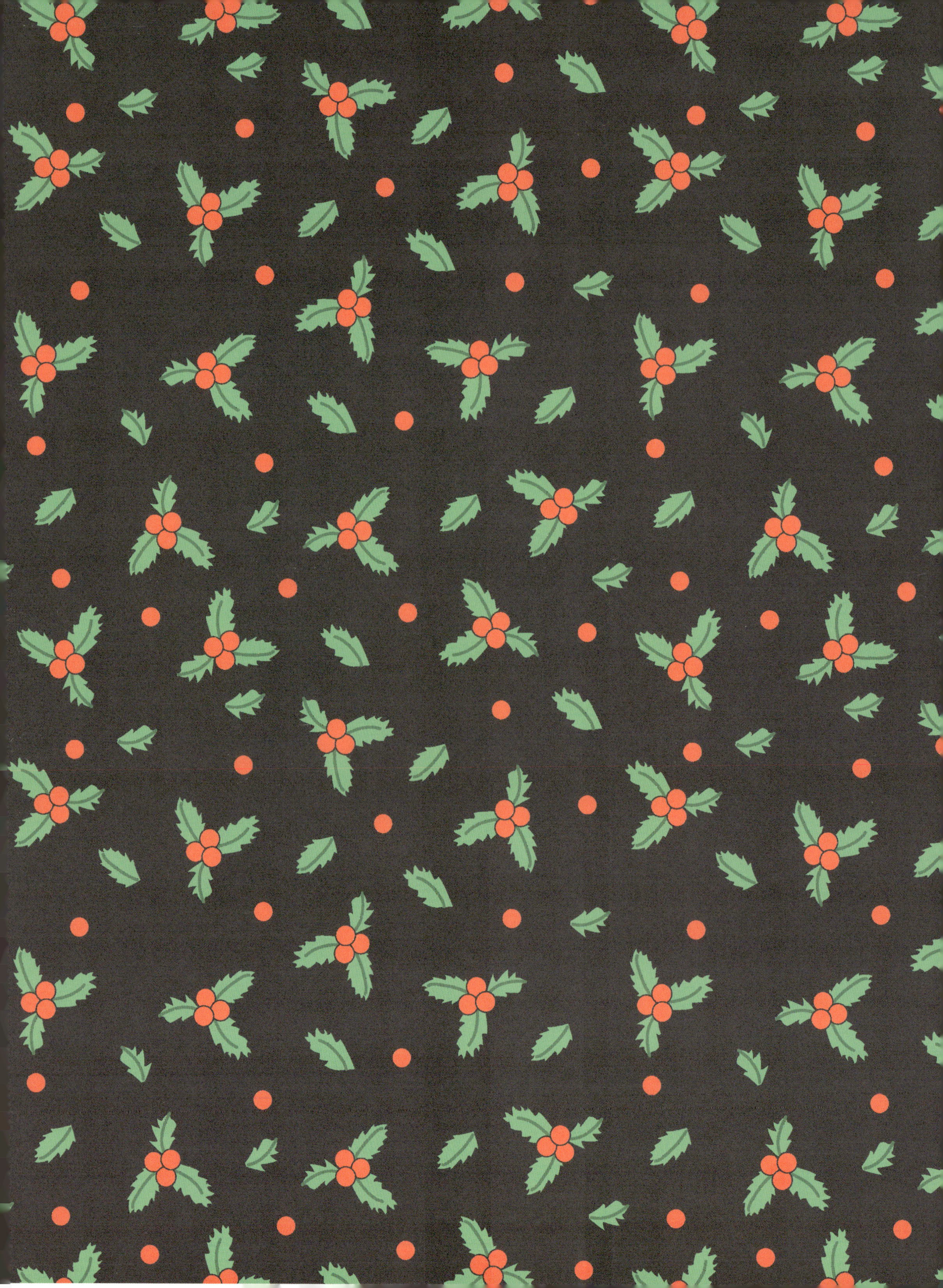

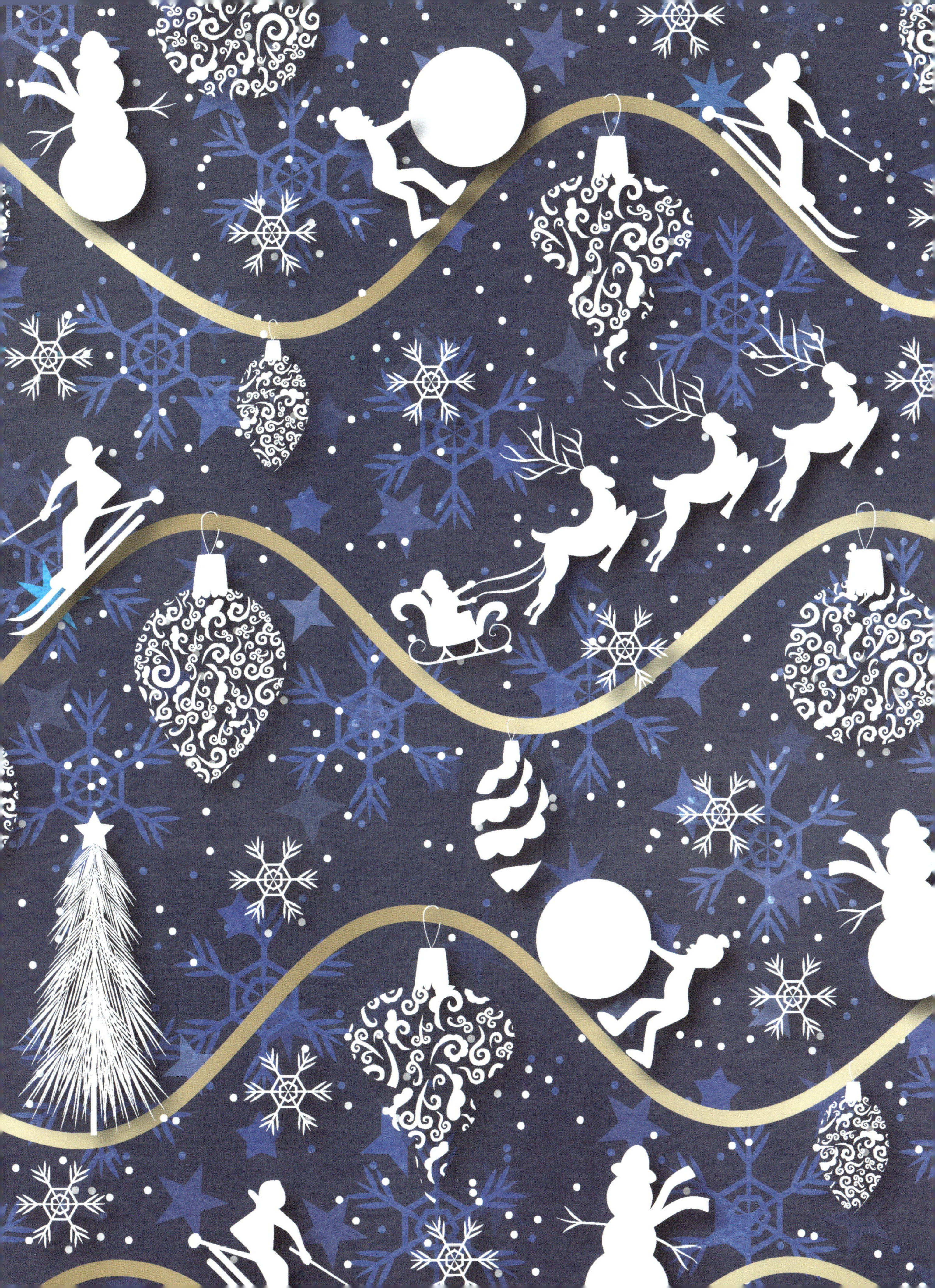

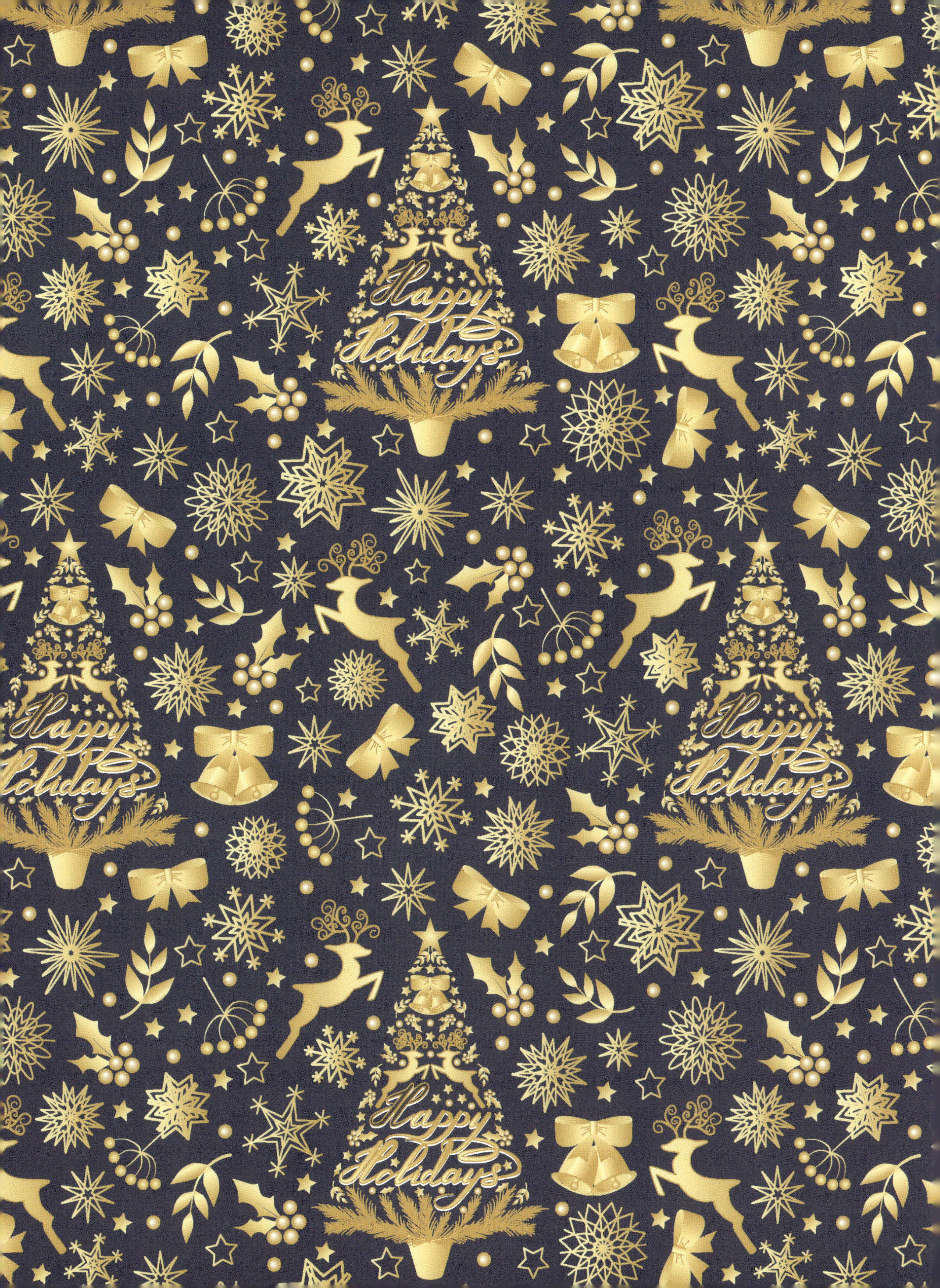
Happy Holidays
Happy Holidays
Happy Holidays
Happy Holidays

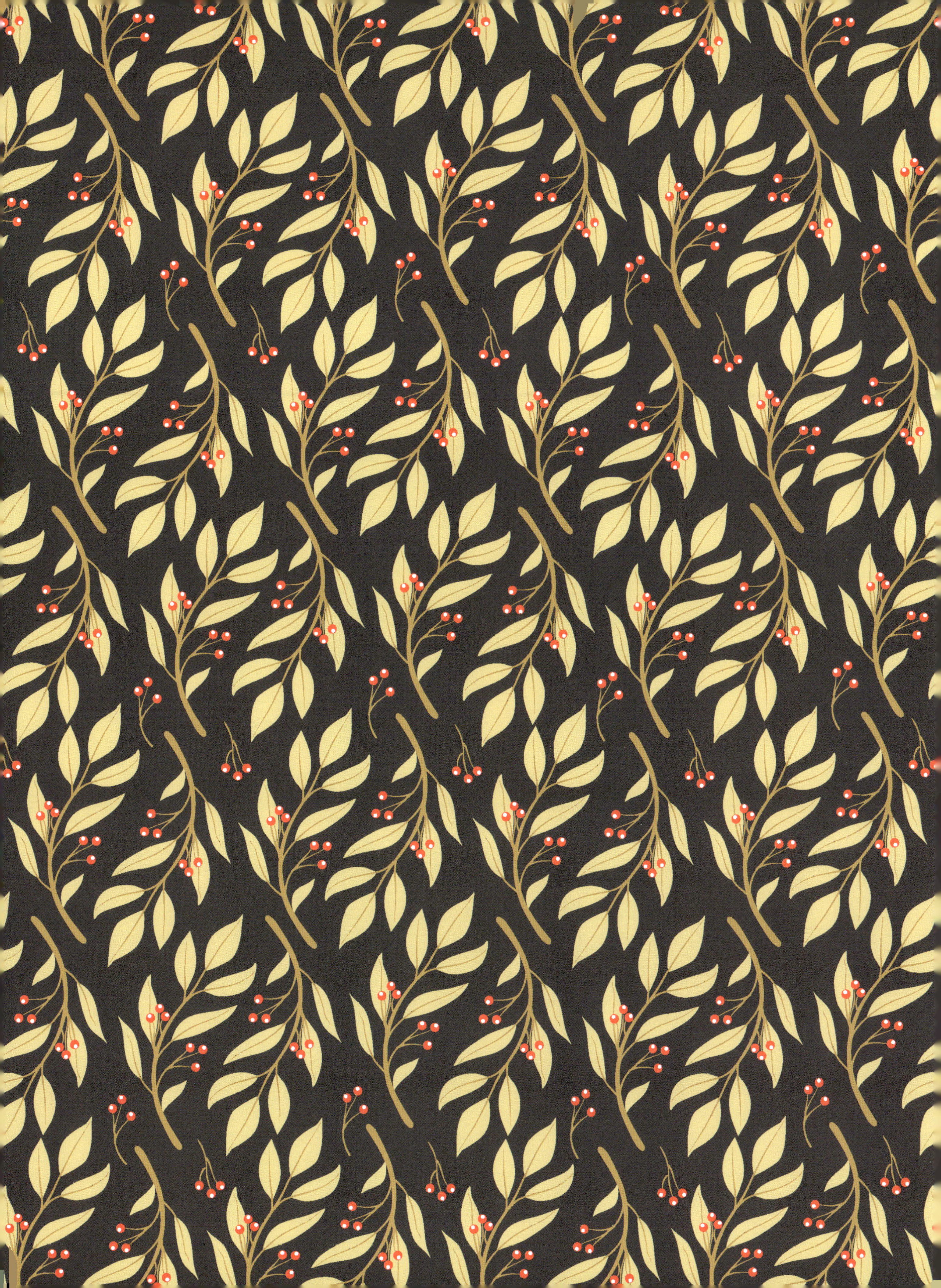

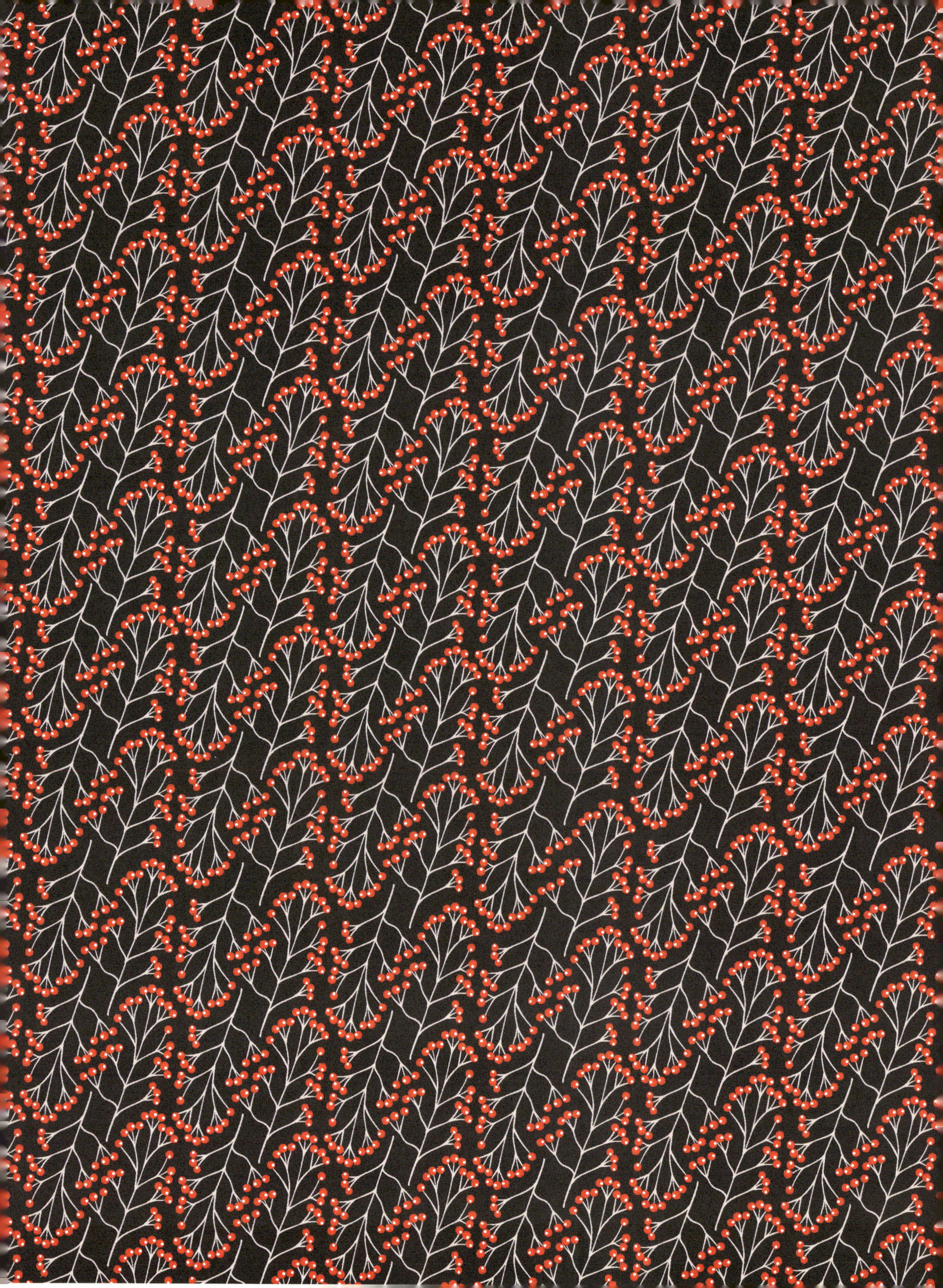

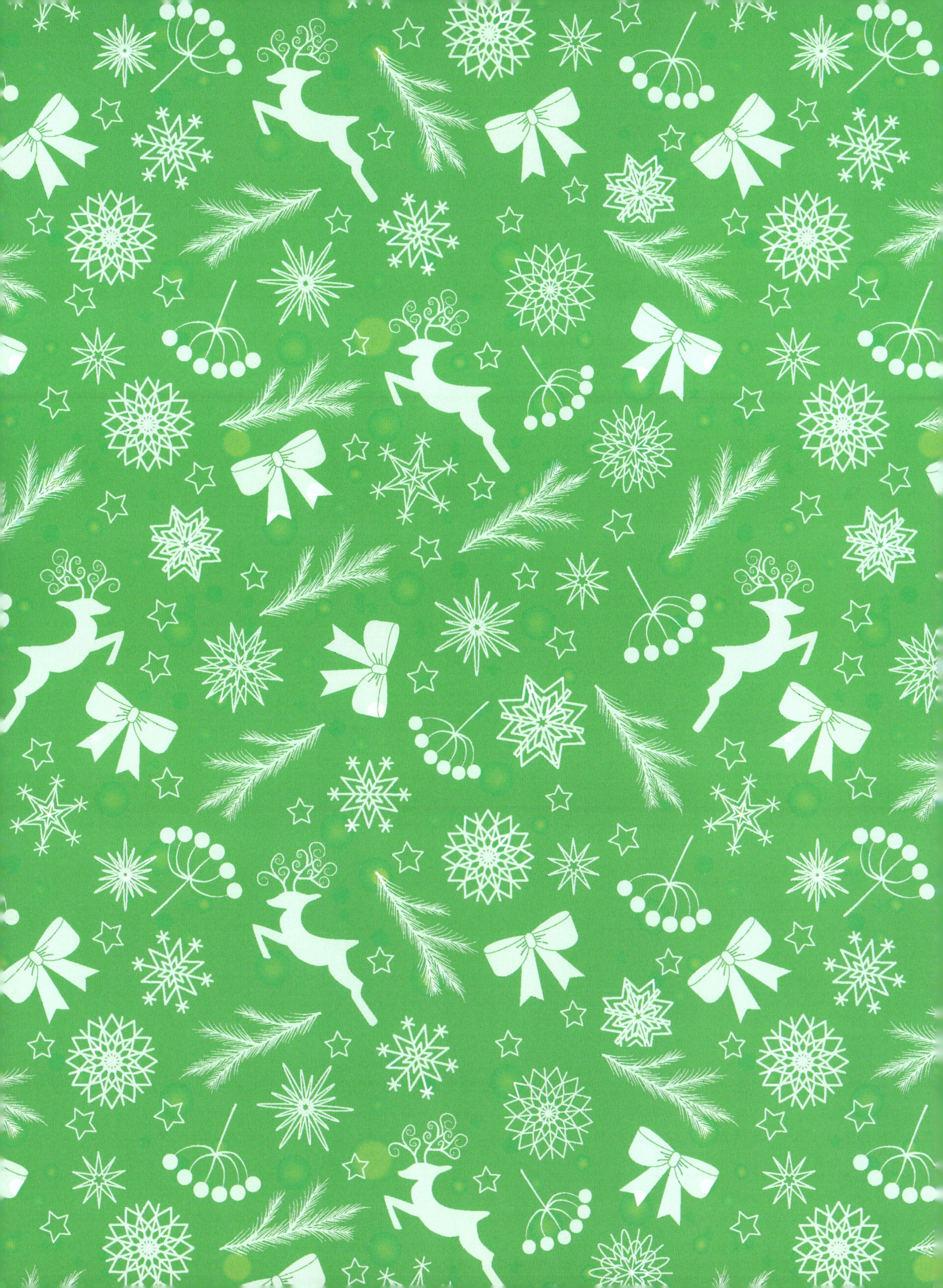

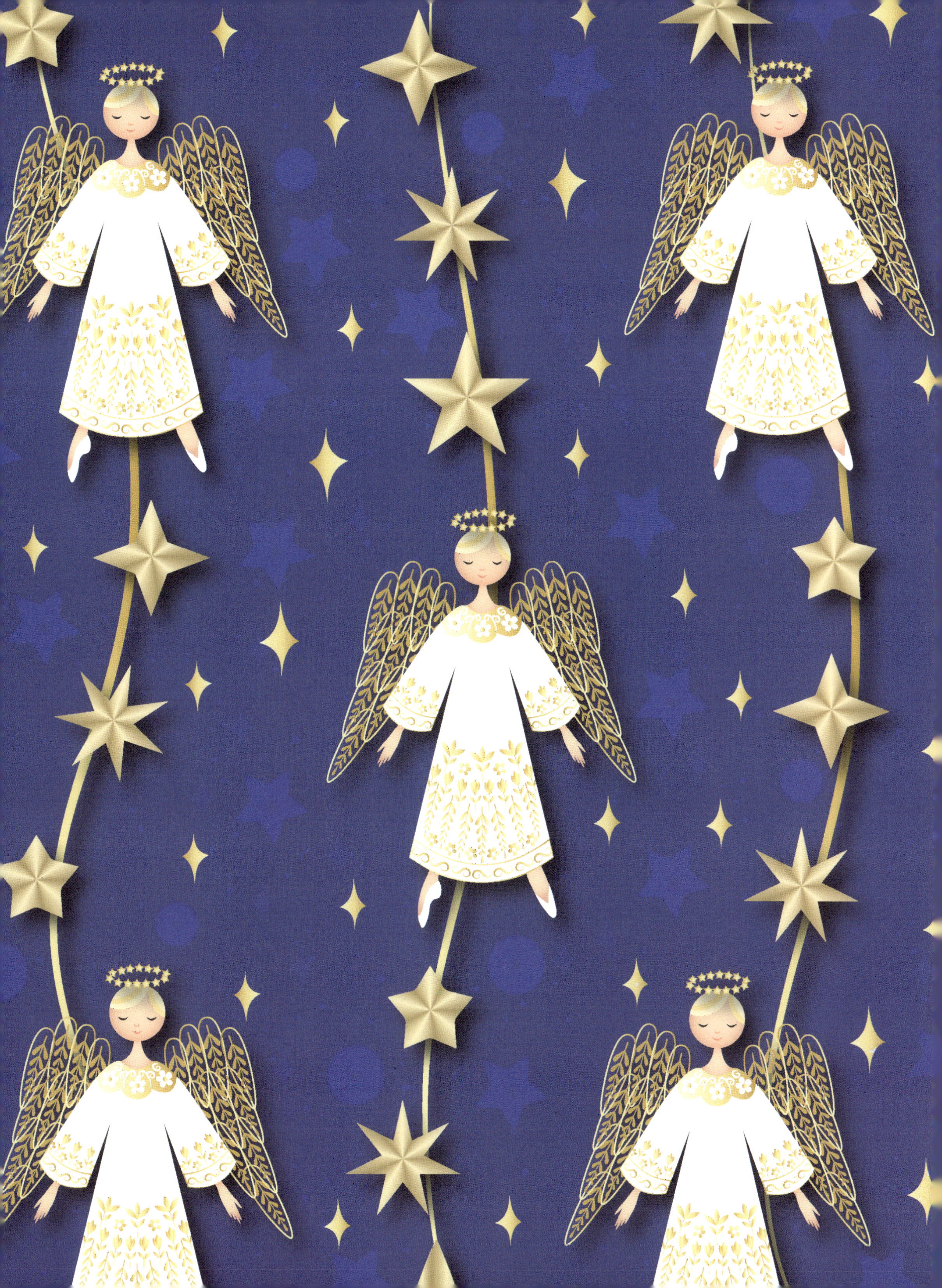

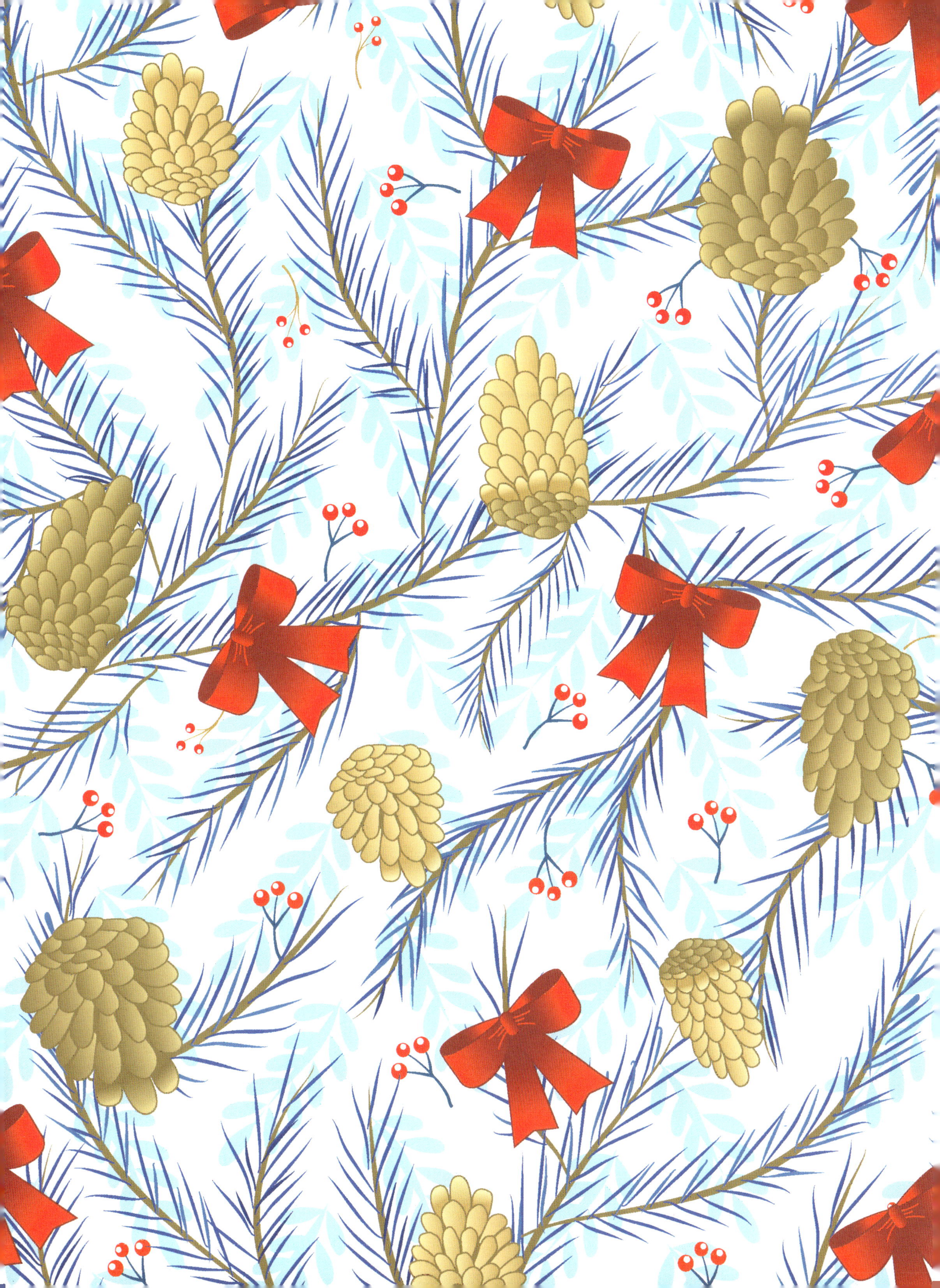

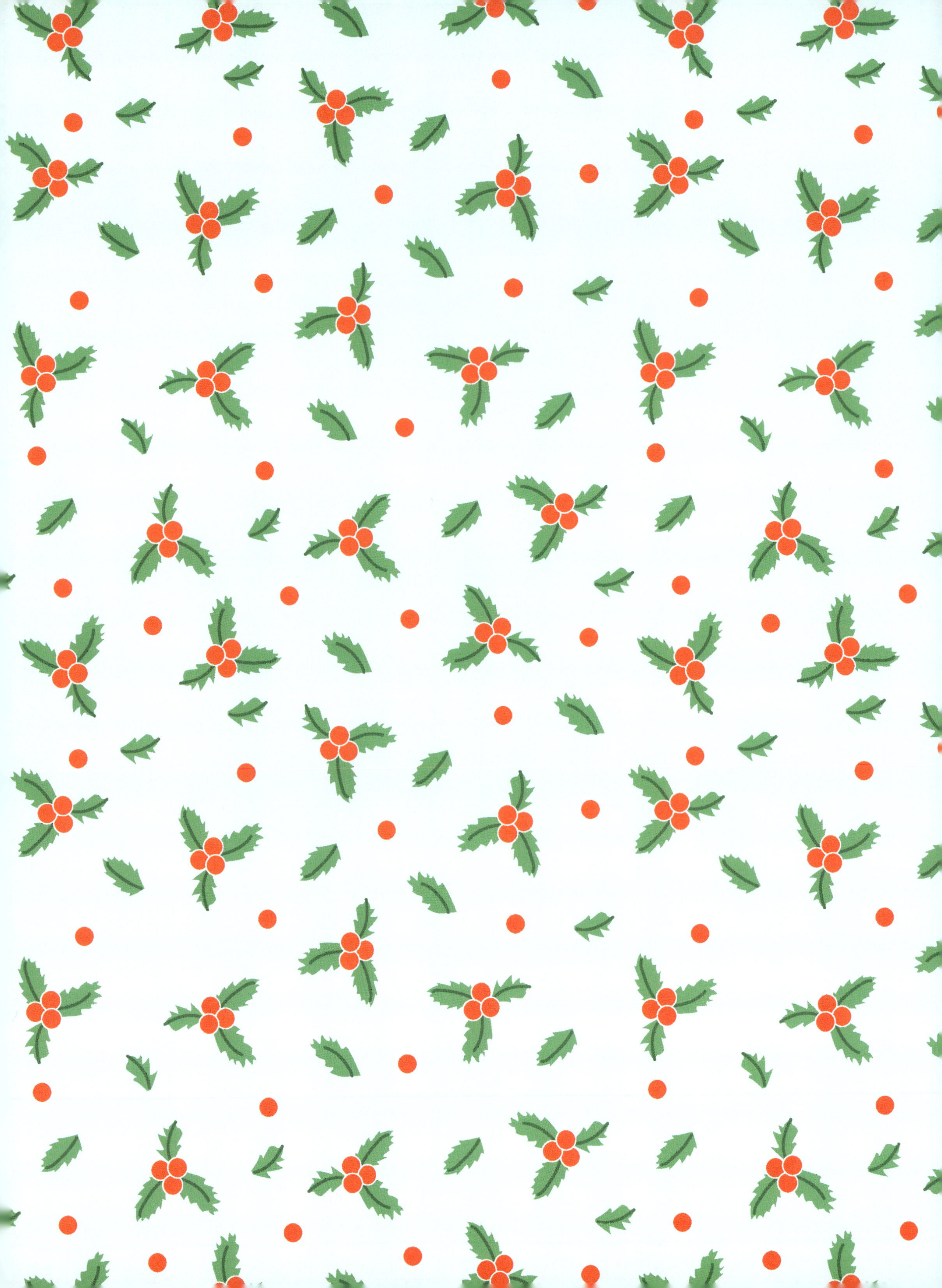

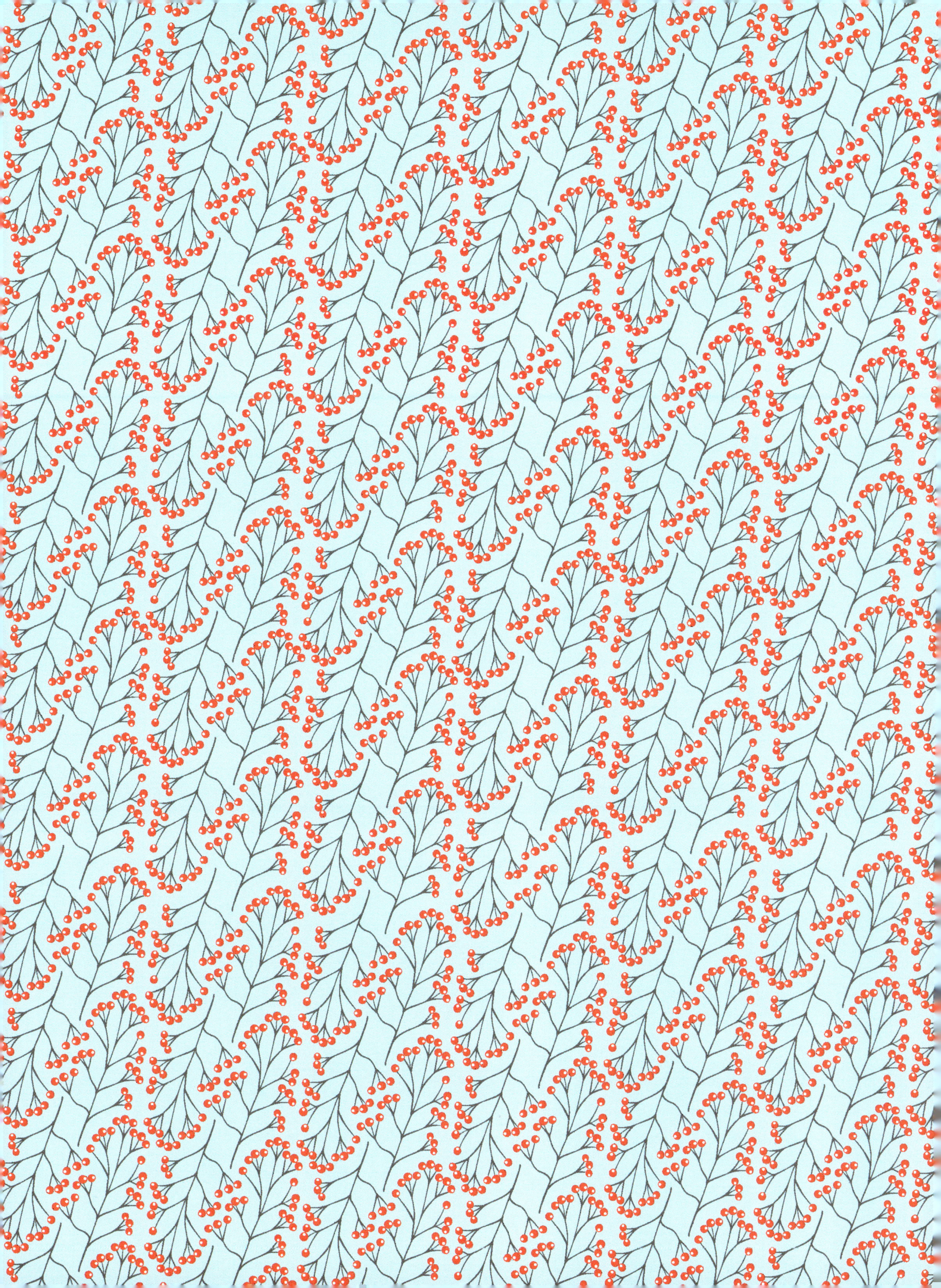

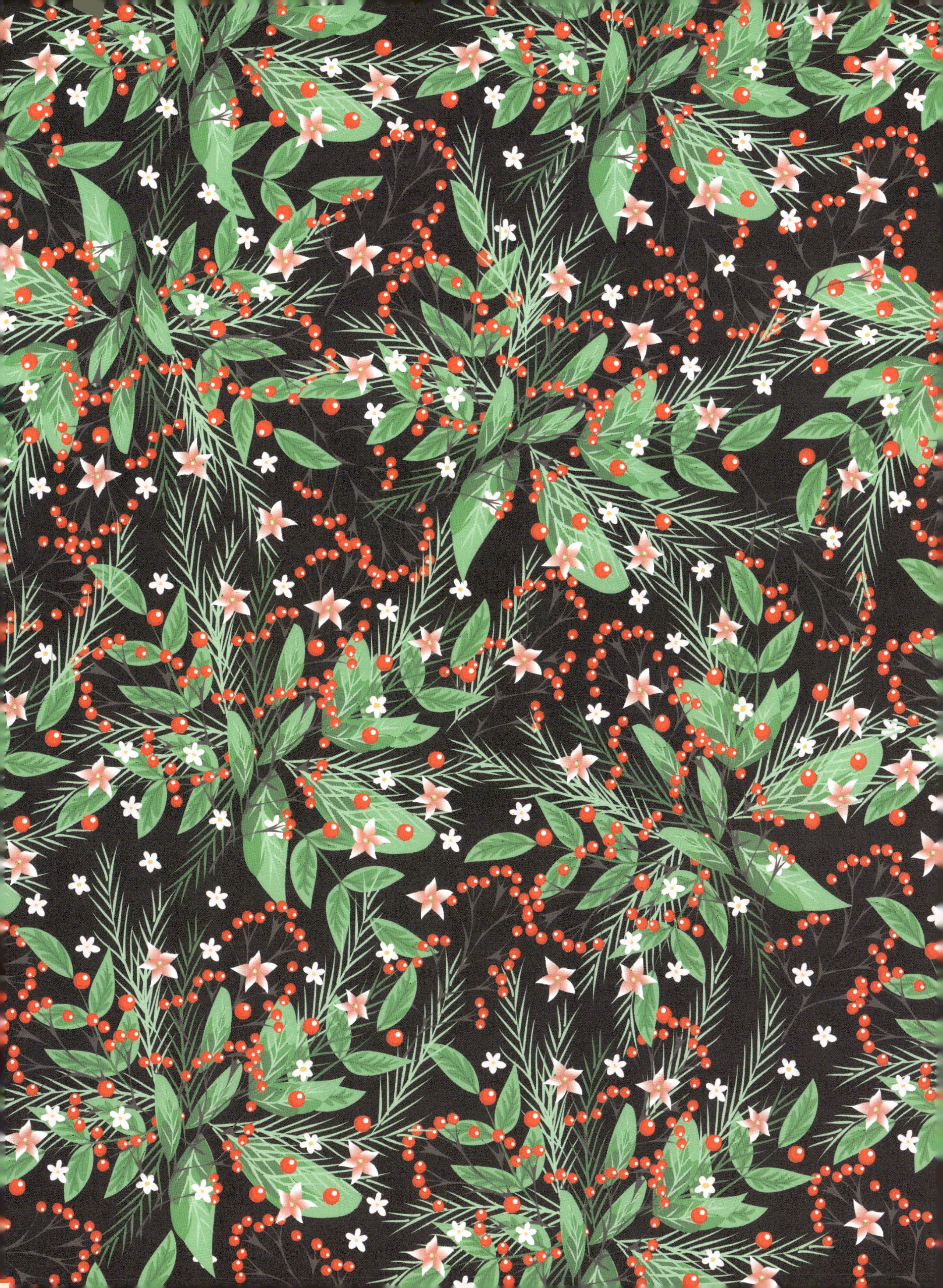

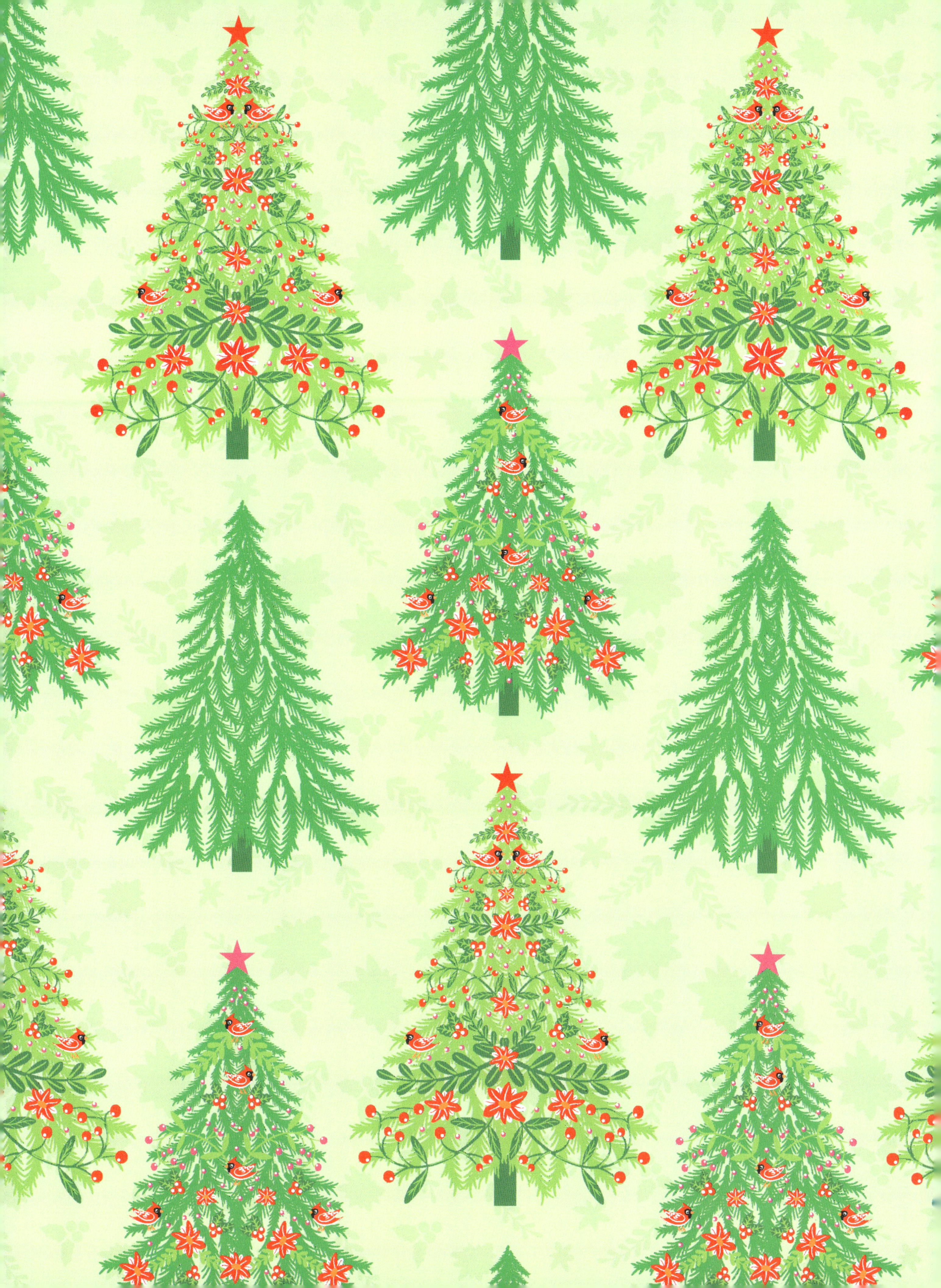

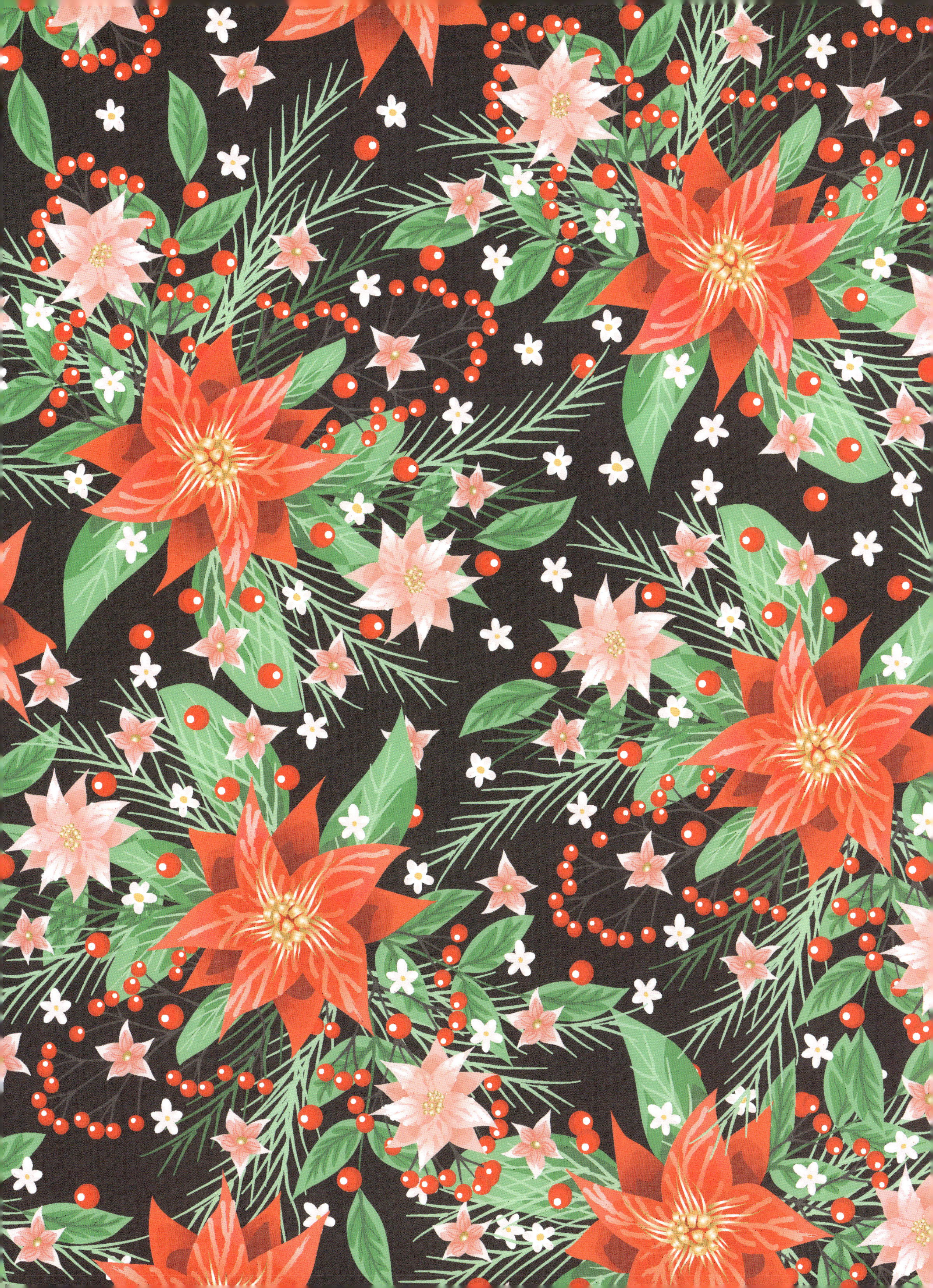

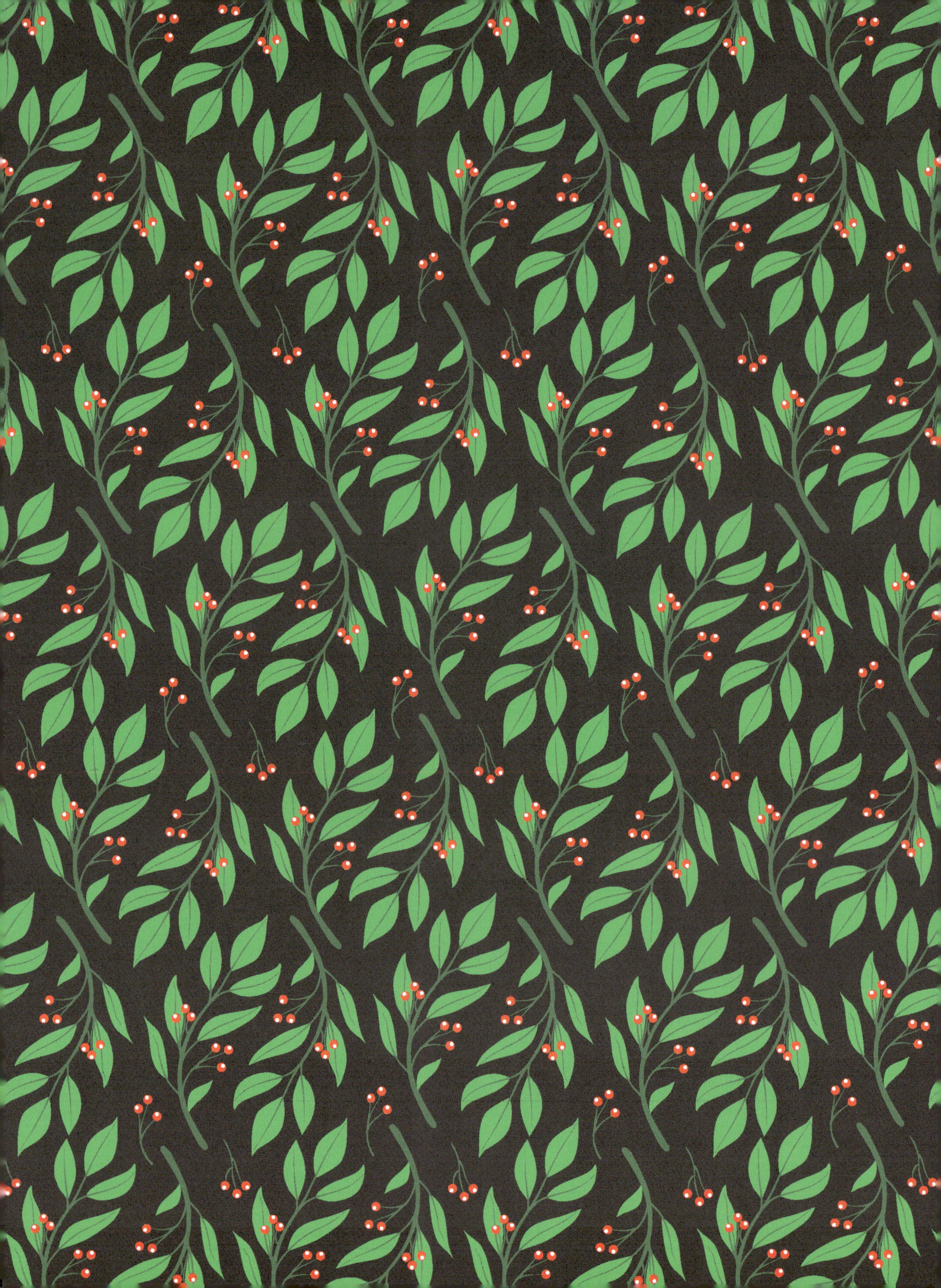

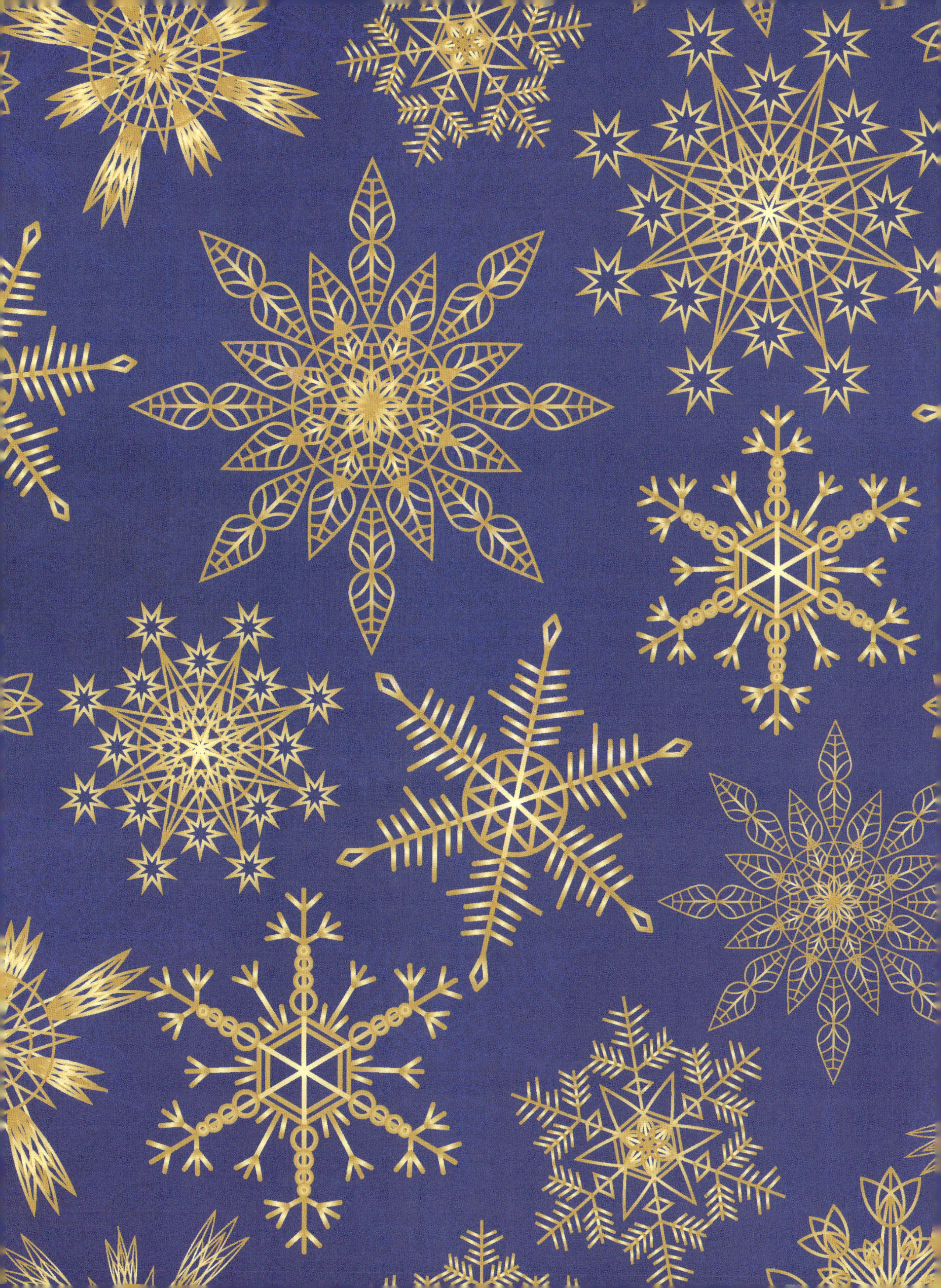

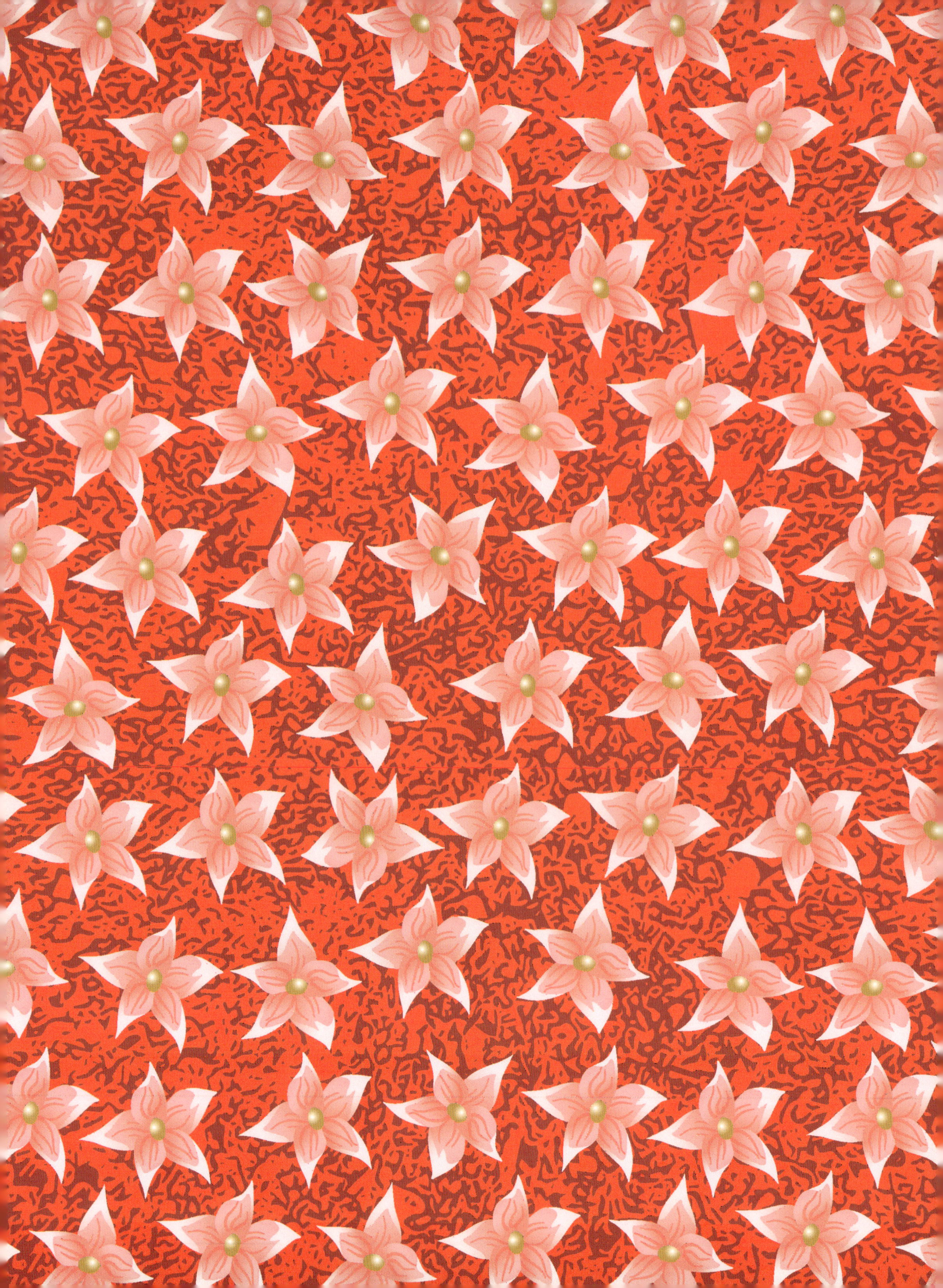

Printed in Great Britain
by Amazon

74975064R00024